The Big Run
and
Get Off!

Level 2 – Red

Helpful Hints for Reading at Home

The graphemes (written letters) and phonemes (units of sound) used throughout this series are aligned with Letters and Sounds. This offers a consistent approach to learning whether reading at home or in the classroom.

HERE IS A LIST OF PHONEMES FOR THIS PHASE OF LEARNING. AN EXAMPLE OF THE PRONUNCIATION CAN BE FOUND IN BRACKETS.

Phase 2			
s (sat)	a (cat)	t (tap)	p (tap)
i (pin)	n (net)	m (man)	d (dog)
g (go)	o (sock)	c (cat)	k (kin)
ck (sack)	e (elf)	u (up)	r (rabbit)
h (hut)	b (ball)	f (fish)	ff (off)
l (lip)	ll (ball)	ss (hiss)	

HERE ARE SOME WORDS WHICH YOUR CHILD MAY FIND TRICKY.

Phase 2 Tricky Words			
the	to	I	no
go	into		

TOP TIPS FOR HELPING YOUR CHILD TO READ:

- Allow children time to break down unfamiliar words into units of sound and then encourage children to string these sounds together to create the word.

- Encourage your child to point out any focus phonics when they are used.

- Read through the book more than once to grow confidence.

- Ask simple questions about the text to assess understanding.

- Encourage children to use illustrations as prompts.

This book focuses on the phonemes /f/ and /ff/ and is a red level 2 book band.

The Big Fan
and
Get Off!

Written by
William Anthony

Illustrated by
Gareth Liddington

Can you make it through the maze to collect the sound f? How many objects containing f can you collect along the way?

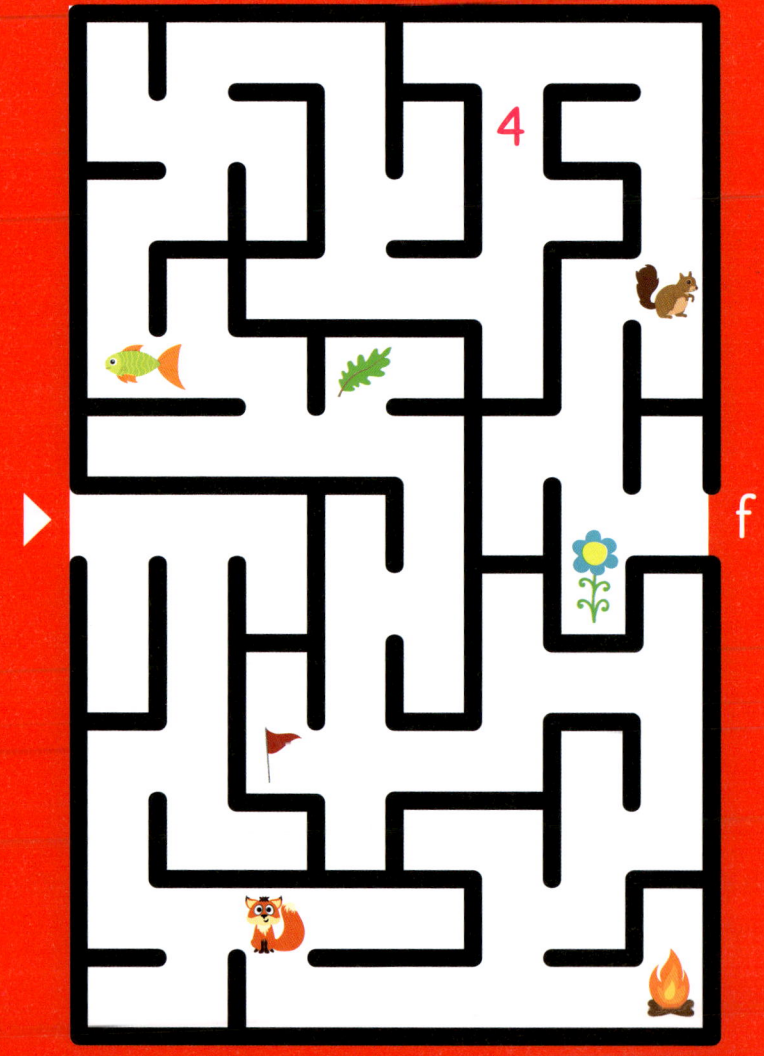

The Big Fan

Written by
William Anthony

Illustrated by
Gareth Liddington

Meg is at the top.

Meg is a big fan.

It is the kick off.

Go go go!

It is in the net!

Meg is up. It is fun!

The ref can pip.

The fans get on.

Meg can run and kick.

It is a fab kick. It is in!

Meg did it!

Meg has a lot of fun as a fan.

Can you say this sound and draw it with your finger?

Get Off!

Written by
William Anthony

Illustrated by
Gareth Liddington

The dog is on the fan.

"Get off!" huffs Dad.

The dog is on the top.

"Get off!" huffs Dad.

Dad is in a faff.

Dad has to go!

The dog has got the muff.

"Get off!" huffs Dad.

The dog is on the figs.

"Get off!" huffs Dad.

Dad gets it!
"Ruff ruff!"

The dog is fed. Dad can go.

©2022 **BookLife Publishing Ltd.**
King's Lynn, Norfolk, PE30 4LS, UK

ISBN 978-1-80155-799-3

All rights reserved. Printed in Poland.
A catalogue record for this book is available from the British Library.

The Big Fan and Get Off!
Written by William Anthony
Illustrated by Gareth Liddington

An Introduction to BookLife Readers...

Our Readers have been specifically created in line with the London Institute of Education's approach to book banding and are phonetically decodable and ordered to support each phase of Letters and Sounds.

Each book has been created to provide the best possible reading and learning experience. Our aim is to share our love of books with children, providing both emerging readers and prolific page-turners with beautiful books that are guaranteed to provoke interest and learning, regardless of ability.

BOOK BAND GRADED using the Institute of Education's approach to levelling.

PHONETICALLY DECODABLE supporting each phase of Letters and Sounds.

EXERCISES AND QUESTIONS to offer reinforcement and to ascertain comprehension.

BEAUTIFULLY ILLUSTRATED to inspire and provoke engagement, providing a variety of styles for the reader to enjoy whilst reading through the series.

AUTHOR INSIGHT:
WILLIAM ANTHONY

William Anthony's involvement with children's education is quite extensive. He has written over 60 titles with BookLife Publishing so far, across a wide range of subjects. William graduated from Cardiff University with a 1st Class BA (Hons) in Journalism, Media and Culture, creating an app and a TV series, among other things, during his time there.

William Anthony has also produced work for the Prince's Trust, a charity created by HRH The Prince of Wales, that helps young people with their professional future. He has created animated videos for a children's education company that works closely with the charity.

This book focuses on the phonemes /f/ and /ff/ and is a red level 2 book band.